DAILY Q&A

A JOURNAL FOR POSITIVITY, KINDNESS, AND PRODUCTIVITY

MICKEY REED

Daily Q&A: A Journal for Positivity, Kindness, and Productivity
The Teens Edition
Copyright © 2017 Mickey Reed / Michelle Kampmeier / Choose Love Ink

All rights reserved.

This book contains material protected under International and Federal Copyright Laws and Treaties. Any unauthorized reprint or use of this material is prohibited. No part of this book may be reproduced or transmitted in any form or by any means, electronic or mechanical, including photocopying, recording, or by an information and retrieval system without express written permission from the author, except for the brief quotation in a book review.

ISBN: 9781981719853
Cover Design: Josh Kampmeier
Cover Image: o_april / blue67 | depositphotos
Formatting: Josh Kampmeier / Michelle Kampmeier

Why a Daily Q&A Journal?

Checking in with yourself each day is important. It can help you stay focused, positive, and happy. Journaling is a great way to track your feelings, your patterns in mood and emotions, and your progress toward achieving your goals.

The questions in this journal will help you focus on positivity, kindness, and productivity in your teen years. Each question should let you know if you got the most out of your day, practiced gratitude, and concentrated on the positive side of things. If you didn't, they will encourage you to try again tomorrow.

Completing This Journal

Set your goals

If you don't know what your goals are, take some time to think about what you want to achieve. Start small (attending certain classes, doing your homework, making time for hobbies, getting a job) and work your way up (graduating with honors, getting into your dream school, winning extracurricular activities competitions). Once you've decided on your goals, write them down in the space provided. This is so important to your progress. When they're real, on paper, somewhere you can see them often, you'll keep them in your mind. Staying aware of them will lead to more success.

Be honest

Be honest with yourself. Write your true feelings. No one else has to see the pages of this journal, so it's a judgment-free zone. You can answer the questions openly. The only way you can achieve personal growth is by being truthful about your thoughts, feelings, and experiences. So fill these pages with honesty, check in with yourself daily, and learn from each day.

Enjoy the process

Have fun with this, and practice kindness with yourself. Easily forgive yourself if you miss a day or can't answer every question each time you check in. The hope is that you'll look forward to answering the questions and be more aware of things you'll be able to write in this journal during the day. Each day, search for things to smile about, be grateful for, or do for yourself and others.

30-Day Check-In

Every 30 pages, there is a different kind of check-in. You'll review your progress for the last 30 days, gauge how your goals are coming along, and assess your eye for positivity and kindness. Are your goals different than they were a month ago? Are you using time wisely and accomplishing your objectives? Are you noticing more kindness and positivity in your life? Make notes to track your overall monthly growth and development here.

Questions in the Journal

Date / Mood / Song of the Day

Write the day's date, your overall mood, and your "song of the day." The song can be one you particularly enjoyed that day or one that describes your day. If you had a different source of entertainment that made you happy that day, feel free to share that instead. Maybe you watched your favorite movie or played a game you love instead.

Name three things you're grateful for.

This section is for you to list three different things you were thankful for that day. They don't have to be different each day, but try to think outside the box on this one. The point is to dig deep and find gratitude in everything.

How was school today? And your extracurriculars?

Write a few sentences that summarize your day. Did you participate in your classes? Are you upset with the amount of homework you got? Did you have a meeting for your chosen club or team sport? How'd it all go? Be honest and track how you feel. If it's the weekend or a day off from school, write about your day in general.

Who did you compliment today? And what did you say?

Compliments breed happiness, and happiness breeds positivity and kindness. That's what this journal is all about, so compliment someone each day, even if it's something really small. Everyone loves hearing something good about themselves, and hopefully they'll pay it forward.

What is the best thing that happened?

Did you make a new friend? Get an A on your test? Score the winning point for your team? Reflect on the day and record your favorite thing(s). And smile. ☺

How will you make tomorrow awesome?

Do you have plans for the next day? How can you make the best of those? Write down ways you can prepare to have the best day ever and then make them happen. Or make notes here about future assignments, to-do items, etc. Staying organized is key.

Doodle something fun.

Draw anything your heart desires in the space here—even if it's just a scribble. Creativity fosters positivity, so have fun with this with any medium you want. Don't get discouraged if you're not an artist—it says "doodle" for a reason. But feel free to bust out markers, crayons, colored pencils, pens, or anything else you want to draw with and let loose.

Goals

Use this page to record your goals. No dream is too big. But you also need a plan to achieve these goals. What has to happen in order to make these goals a reality? Do you need to find a job? Save money? Network and make connections? Make more time after school? Add all of your goals to the space below to stay on track. And check back often to see if they have changed over time.

Short-Term Goals:

1.

2.

3.

4.

5.

Long-Term Goals:

1.

2.

3.

4.

5.

Steps I Need To Take:

Date: 6/14/18
Mood: Neutral
Song of the Day: N/A

Name three things you're grateful for:

1. games
2. Bikes
3. TV

How was school today? And your extracurriculars?

N/A

Who did you compliment today? And what did you say?

Caleb, House in game looked nice

What is the best thing that happened?

rode bikes along route

How will you make tomorrow awesome?

Try to avoid conflict

Doodle something fun:

Date: 6/15/18
Mood: Great
Song of the Day: N/A

Name three things you're grateful for:

1. Pizza
2. Family
3. Cars

How was school today? And your extracurriculars?

N/A

Who did you compliment today? And what did you say?

N/A

What is the best thing that happened?

Riding the train and watching the steam assembly

How will you make tomorrow awesome?

Be in a good mood

Doodle something fun:

Date: 6/16/19
Mood: Neutral
Song of the Day: N/A

Name three things you're grateful for:

1. CO_2
2. O_2
3. Bags

How was school today? And your extracurriculars?

N/A

Who did you compliment today? And what did you say?

N/A

What is the best thing that happened?

we went to Kings island

How will you make tomorrow awesome?

Be nice

Doodle something fun:

Date:

Mood:

Song of the Day:

Name three things you're grateful for:

    1.

    2.

    3.

How was school today? And your extracurriculars?

Who did you compliment today? And what did you say?

What is the best thing that happened?

How will you make tomorrow awesome?

Doodle something fun:

Date:

Mood:

Song of the Day:

Name three things you're grateful for:

    1.

    2.

    3.

How was school today? And your extracurriculars?

Who did you compliment today? And what did you say?

What is the best thing that happened?

How will you make tomorrow awesome?

Doodle something fun:

Date:

Mood:

Song of the Day:

Name three things you're grateful for:

    1.

    2.

    3.

How was school today? And your extracurriculars?

Who did you compliment today? And what did you say?

What is the best thing that happened?

How will you make tomorrow awesome?

Doodle something fun:

Date:

Mood:

Song of the Day:

Name three things you're grateful for:

    1.

    2.

    3.

How was school today? And your extracurriculars?

Who did you compliment today? And what did you say?

What is the best thing that happened?

How will you make tomorrow awesome?

Doodle something fun:

Date:

Mood:

Song of the Day:

Name three things you're grateful for:

    1.

    2.

    3.

How was school today? And your extracurriculars?

Who did you compliment today? And what did you say?

What is the best thing that happened?

How will you make tomorrow awesome?

Doodle something fun:

Date:

Mood:

Song of the Day:

Name three things you're grateful for:

    1.

    2.

    3.

How was school today? And your extracurriculars?

Who did you compliment today? And what did you say?

What is the best thing that happened?

How will you make tomorrow awesome?

Doodle something fun:

Date:

Mood:

Song of the Day:

Name three things you're grateful for:

    1.

    2.

    3.

How was school today? And your extracurriculars?

Who did you compliment today? And what did you say?

What is the best thing that happened?

How will you make tomorrow awesome?

Doodle something fun:

Date:

Mood:

Song of the Day:

Name three things you're grateful for:

    1.

    2.

    3.

How was school today? And your extracurriculars?

Who did you compliment today? And what did you say?

What is the best thing that happened?

How will you make tomorrow awesome?

Doodle something fun:

Date:

Mood:

Song of the Day:

Name three things you're grateful for:

    1.

    2.

    3.

How was school today? And your extracurriculars?

Who did you compliment today? And what did you say?

What is the best thing that happened?

How will you make tomorrow awesome?

Doodle something fun:

Date:

Mood:

Song of the Day:

Name three things you're grateful for:

    1.

    2.

    3.

How was school today? And your extracurriculars?

Who did you compliment today? And what did you say?

What is the best thing that happened?

How will you make tomorrow awesome?

Doodle something fun:

Date:

Mood:

Song of the Day:

Name three things you're grateful for:

    1.

    2.

    3.

How was school today? And your extracurriculars?

Who did you compliment today? And what did you say?

What is the best thing that happened?

How will you make tomorrow awesome?

Doodle something fun:

Date:

Mood:

Song of the Day:

Name three things you're grateful for:

    1.

    2.

    3.

How was school today? And your extracurriculars?

Who did you compliment today? And what did you say?

What is the best thing that happened?

How will you make tomorrow awesome?

Doodle something fun:

Date:

Mood:

Song of the Day:

Name three things you're grateful for:

    1.

    2.

    3.

How was school today? And your extracurriculars?

Who did you compliment today? And what did you say?

What is the best thing that happened?

How will you make tomorrow awesome?

Doodle something fun:

Date:

Mood:

Song of the Day:

Name three things you're grateful for:

1.

2.

3.

How was school today? And your extracurriculars?

Who did you compliment today? And what did you say?

What is the best thing that happened?

How will you make tomorrow awesome?

Doodle something fun:

Date:

Mood:

Song of the Day:

Name three things you're grateful for:

1.

2.

3.

How was school today? And your extracurriculars?

Who did you compliment today? And what did you say?

What is the best thing that happened?

How will you make tomorrow awesome?

Doodle something fun:

Date:

Mood:

Song of the Day:

Name three things you're grateful for:

1.

2.

3.

How was school today? And your extracurriculars?

Who did you compliment today? And what did you say?

What is the best thing that happened?

How will you make tomorrow awesome?

Doodle something fun:

Date:

Mood:

Song of the Day:

Name three things you're grateful for:

    1.

    2.

    3.

How was school today? And your extracurriculars?

Who did you compliment today? And what did you say?

What is the best thing that happened?

How will you make tomorrow awesome?

Doodle something fun:

Date:

Mood:

Song of the Day:

Name three things you're grateful for:

    1.

    2.

    3.

How was school today? And your extracurriculars?

Who did you compliment today? And what did you say?

What is the best thing that happened?

How will you make tomorrow awesome?

Doodle something fun:

Date:

Mood:

Song of the Day:

Name three things you're grateful for:

    1.

    2.

    3.

How was school today? And your extracurriculars?

Who did you compliment today? And what did you say?

What is the best thing that happened?

How will you make tomorrow awesome?

Doodle something fun:

Date:

Mood:

Song of the Day:

Name three things you're grateful for:

    1.

    2.

    3.

How was school today? And your extracurriculars?

Who did you compliment today? And what did you say?

What is the best thing that happened?

How will you make tomorrow awesome?

Doodle something fun:

Date:

Mood:

Song of the Day:

Name three things you're grateful for:

    1.

    2.

    3.

How was school today? And your extracurriculars?

Who did you compliment today? And what did you say?

What is the best thing that happened?

How will you make tomorrow awesome?

Doodle something fun:

Date:

Mood:

Song of the Day:

Name three things you're grateful for:

    1.

    2.

    3.

How was school today? And your extracurriculars?

Who did you compliment today? And what did you say?

What is the best thing that happened?

How will you make tomorrow awesome?

Doodle something fun:

Date:

Mood:

Song of the Day:

Name three things you're grateful for:

    1.

    2.

    3.

How was school today? And your extracurriculars?

Who did you compliment today? And what did you say?

What is the best thing that happened?

How will you make tomorrow awesome?

Doodle something fun:

Date:

Mood:

Song of the Day:

Name three things you're grateful for:

1.

2.

3.

How was school today? And your extracurriculars?

Who did you compliment today? And what did you say?

What is the best thing that happened?

How will you make tomorrow awesome?

Doodle something fun:

Date:

Mood:

Song of the Day:

Name three things you're grateful for:

1.

2.

3.

How was school today? And your extracurriculars?

Who did you compliment today? And what did you say?

What is the best thing that happened?

How will you make tomorrow awesome?

Doodle something fun:

Date:

Mood:

Song of the Day:

Name three things you're grateful for:

    1.

    2.

    3.

How was school today? And your extracurriculars?

Who did you compliment today? And what did you say?

What is the best thing that happened?

How will you make tomorrow awesome?

Doodle something fun:

Date:

Mood:

Song of the Day:

Name three things you're grateful for:

    1.

    2.

    3.

How was school today? And your extracurriculars?

Who did you compliment today? And what did you say?

What is the best thing that happened?

How will you make tomorrow awesome?

Doodle something fun:

30-Day Check-In

Date:

Best thing that happened in the last 30 days:

Have you spent time working toward your goals?

How have your goals changed over the last 30 days?

Are you satisfied with the progress you've made?

How have you felt this month compared to last month?

What do you hope to accomplish in the next 30 days?

What can you do in the next 30 days to accomplish those things?

Date:

Mood:

Song of the Day:

Name three things you're grateful for:

    1.

    2.

    3.

How was school today? And your extracurriculars?

Who did you compliment today? And what did you say?

What is the best thing that happened?

How will you make tomorrow awesome?

Doodle something fun:

Date:

Mood:

Song of the Day:

Name three things you're grateful for:

    1.

    2.

    3.

How was school today? And your extracurriculars?

Who did you compliment today? And what did you say?

What is the best thing that happened?

How will you make tomorrow awesome?

Doodle something fun:

Date:

Mood:

Song of the Day:

Name three things you're grateful for:

    1.

    2.

    3.

How was school today? And your extracurriculars?

Who did you compliment today? And what did you say?

What is the best thing that happened?

How will you make tomorrow awesome?

Doodle something fun:

Date:

Mood:

Song of the Day:

Name three things you're grateful for:

1.

2.

3.

How was school today? And your extracurriculars?

Who did you compliment today? And what did you say?

What is the best thing that happened?

How will you make tomorrow awesome?

Doodle something fun:

Date:

Mood:

Song of the Day:

Name three things you're grateful for:

    1.

    2.

    3.

How was school today? And your extracurriculars?

Who did you compliment today? And what did you say?

What is the best thing that happened?

How will you make tomorrow awesome?

Doodle something fun:

Date:

Mood:

Song of the Day:

Name three things you're grateful for:

1.

2.

3.

How was school today? And your extracurriculars?

Who did you compliment today? And what did you say?

What is the best thing that happened?

How will you make tomorrow awesome?

Doodle something fun:

Date:

Mood:

Song of the Day:

Name three things you're grateful for:

1.

2.

3.

How was school today? And your extracurriculars?

Who did you compliment today? And what did you say?

What is the best thing that happened?

How will you make tomorrow awesome?

Doodle something fun:

Date:

Mood:

Song of the Day:

Name three things you're grateful for:

1.

2.

3.

How was school today? And your extracurriculars?

Who did you compliment today? And what did you say?

What is the best thing that happened?

How will you make tomorrow awesome?

Doodle something fun:

Date:

Mood:

Song of the Day:

Name three things you're grateful for:

1.

2.

3.

How was school today? And your extracurriculars?

Who did you compliment today? And what did you say?

What is the best thing that happened?

How will you make tomorrow awesome?

Doodle something fun:

Date:

Mood:

Song of the Day:

Name three things you're grateful for:

    1.

    2.

    3.

How was school today? And your extracurriculars?

Who did you compliment today? And what did you say?

What is the best thing that happened?

How will you make tomorrow awesome?

Doodle something fun:

Date:

Mood:

Song of the Day:

Name three things you're grateful for:

    1.

    2.

    3.

How was school today? And your extracurriculars?

Who did you compliment today? And what did you say?

What is the best thing that happened?

How will you make tomorrow awesome?

Doodle something fun:

Date:

Mood:

Song of the Day:

Name three things you're grateful for:

    1.

    2.

    3.

How was school today? And your extracurriculars?

Who did you compliment today? And what did you say?

What is the best thing that happened?

How will you make tomorrow awesome?

Doodle something fun:

Date:

Mood:

Song of the Day:

Name three things you're grateful for:

    1.

    2.

    3.

How was school today? And your extracurriculars?

Who did you compliment today? And what did you say?

What is the best thing that happened?

How will you make tomorrow awesome?

Doodle something fun:

Date:

Mood:

Song of the Day:

Name three things you're grateful for:

    1.

    2.

    3.

How was school today? And your extracurriculars?

Who did you compliment today? And what did you say?

What is the best thing that happened?

How will you make tomorrow awesome?

Doodle something fun:

Date:

Mood:

Song of the Day:

Name three things you're grateful for:

    1.

    2.

    3.

How was school today? And your extracurriculars?

Who did you compliment today? And what did you say?

What is the best thing that happened?

How will you make tomorrow awesome?

Doodle something fun:

Date:

Mood:

Song of the Day:

Name three things you're grateful for:

    1.

    2.

    3.

How was school today? And your extracurriculars?

Who did you compliment today? And what did you say?

What is the best thing that happened?

How will you make tomorrow awesome?

Doodle something fun:

Date:

Mood:

Song of the Day:

Name three things you're grateful for:

    1.

    2.

    3.

How was school today? And your extracurriculars?

Who did you compliment today? And what did you say?

What is the best thing that happened?

How will you make tomorrow awesome?

Doodle something fun:

Date:

Mood:

Song of the Day:

Name three things you're grateful for:

1.

2.

3.

How was school today? And your extracurriculars?

Who did you compliment today? And what did you say?

What is the best thing that happened?

How will you make tomorrow awesome?

Doodle something fun:

Date:

Mood:

Song of the Day:

Name three things you're grateful for:

    1.

    2.

    3.

How was school today? And your extracurriculars?

Who did you compliment today? And what did you say?

What is the best thing that happened?

How will you make tomorrow awesome?

Doodle something fun:

Date:

Mood:

Song of the Day:

Name three things you're grateful for:

1.

2.

3.

How was school today? And your extracurriculars?

Who did you compliment today? And what did you say?

What is the best thing that happened?

How will you make tomorrow awesome?

Doodle something fun:

Date:

Mood:

Song of the Day:

Name three things you're grateful for:

    1.

    2.

    3.

How was school today? And your extracurriculars?

Who did you compliment today? And what did you say?

What is the best thing that happened?

How will you make tomorrow awesome?

Doodle something fun:

Date:

Mood:

Song of the Day:

Name three things you're grateful for:

    1.

    2.

    3.

How was school today? And your extracurriculars?

Who did you compliment today? And what did you say?

What is the best thing that happened?

How will you make tomorrow awesome?

Doodle something fun:

Date:

Mood:

Song of the Day:

Name three things you're grateful for:

    1.

    2.

    3.

How was school today? And your extracurriculars?

Who did you compliment today? And what did you say?

What is the best thing that happened?

How will you make tomorrow awesome?

Doodle something fun:

Date:

Mood:

Song of the Day:

Name three things you're grateful for:

1.

2.

3.

How was school today? And your extracurriculars?

Who did you compliment today? And what did you say?

What is the best thing that happened?

How will you make tomorrow awesome?

Doodle something fun:

Date:

Mood:

Song of the Day:

Name three things you're grateful for:

    1.

    2.

    3.

How was school today? And your extracurriculars?

Who did you compliment today? And what did you say?

What is the best thing that happened?

How will you make tomorrow awesome?

Doodle something fun:

Date:

Mood:

Song of the Day:

Name three things you're grateful for:

    1.

    2.

    3.

How was school today? And your extracurriculars?

Who did you compliment today? And what did you say?

What is the best thing that happened?

How will you make tomorrow awesome?

Doodle something fun:

Date:

Mood:

Song of the Day:

Name three things you're grateful for:

1.

2.

3.

How was school today? And your extracurriculars?

Who did you compliment today? And what did you say?

What is the best thing that happened?

How will you make tomorrow awesome?

Doodle something fun:

Date:

Mood:

Song of the Day:

Name three things you're grateful for:

    1.

    2.

    3.

How was school today? And your extracurriculars?

Who did you compliment today? And what did you say?

What is the best thing that happened?

How will you make tomorrow awesome?

Doodle something fun:

Date:

Mood:

Song of the Day:

Name three things you're grateful for:

    1.

    2.

    3.

How was school today? And your extracurriculars?

Who did you compliment today? And what did you say?

What is the best thing that happened?

How will you make tomorrow awesome?

Doodle something fun:

Date:

Mood:

Song of the Day:

Name three things you're grateful for:

    1.

    2.

    3.

How was school today? And your extracurriculars?

Who did you compliment today? And what did you say?

What is the best thing that happened?

How will you make tomorrow awesome?

Doodle something fun:

30-Day Check-In

Date:

Best thing that happened in the last 30 days:

Have you spent time working toward your goals?

How have your goals changed over the last 30 days?

Are you satisfied with the progress you've made?

How have you felt this month compared to last month?

What do you hope to accomplish in the next 30 days?

What can you do in the next 30 days to accomplish those things?

Date:

Mood:

Song of the Day:

Name three things you're grateful for:

1.

2.

3.

How was school today? And your extracurriculars?

Who did you compliment today? And what did you say?

What is the best thing that happened?

How will you make tomorrow awesome?

Doodle something fun:

Date:

Mood:

Song of the Day:

Name three things you're grateful for:

    1.

    2.

    3.

How was school today? And your extracurriculars?

Who did you compliment today? And what did you say?

What is the best thing that happened?

How will you make tomorrow awesome?

Doodle something fun:

Date:

Mood:

Song of the Day:

Name three things you're grateful for:

    1.

    2.

    3.

How was school today? And your extracurriculars?

Who did you compliment today? And what did you say?

What is the best thing that happened?

How will you make tomorrow awesome?

Doodle something fun:

Date:

Mood:

Song of the Day:

Name three things you're grateful for:

    1.

    2.

    3.

How was school today? And your extracurriculars?

Who did you compliment today? And what did you say?

What is the best thing that happened?

How will you make tomorrow awesome?

Doodle something fun:

Date:

Mood:

Song of the Day:

Name three things you're grateful for:

    1.

    2.

    3.

How was school today? And your extracurriculars?

Who did you compliment today? And what did you say?

What is the best thing that happened?

How will you make tomorrow awesome?

Doodle something fun:

Date:

Mood:

Song of the Day:

Name three things you're grateful for:

    1.

    2.

    3.

How was school today? And your extracurriculars?

Who did you compliment today? And what did you say?

What is the best thing that happened?

How will you make tomorrow awesome?

Doodle something fun:

Date:

Mood:

Song of the Day:

Name three things you're grateful for:

    1.

    2.

    3.

How was school today? And your extracurriculars?

Who did you compliment today? And what did you say?

What is the best thing that happened?

How will you make tomorrow awesome?

Doodle something fun:

Date:

Mood:

Song of the Day:

Name three things you're grateful for:

    1.

    2.

    3.

How was school today? And your extracurriculars?

Who did you compliment today? And what did you say?

What is the best thing that happened?

How will you make tomorrow awesome?

Doodle something fun:

Date:

Mood:

Song of the Day:

Name three things you're grateful for:

    1.

    2.

    3.

How was school today? And your extracurriculars?

Who did you compliment today? And what did you say?

What is the best thing that happened?

How will you make tomorrow awesome?

Doodle something fun:

Date:

Mood:

Song of the Day:

Name three things you're grateful for:

    1.

    2.

    3.

How was school today? And your extracurriculars?

Who did you compliment today? And what did you say?

What is the best thing that happened?

How will you make tomorrow awesome?

Doodle something fun:

Date:

Mood:

Song of the Day:

Name three things you're grateful for:

    1.

    2.

    3.

How was school today? And your extracurriculars?

Who did you compliment today? And what did you say?

What is the best thing that happened?

How will you make tomorrow awesome?

Doodle something fun:

Date:

Mood:

Song of the Day:

Name three things you're grateful for:

1.

2.

3.

How was school today? And your extracurriculars?

Who did you compliment today? And what did you say?

What is the best thing that happened?

How will you make tomorrow awesome?

Doodle something fun:

Date:

Mood:

Song of the Day:

Name three things you're grateful for:

    1.

    2.

    3.

How was school today? And your extracurriculars?

Who did you compliment today? And what did you say?

What is the best thing that happened?

How will you make tomorrow awesome?

Doodle something fun:

Date:

Mood:

Song of the Day:

Name three things you're grateful for:

    1.

    2.

    3.

How was school today? And your extracurriculars?

Who did you compliment today? And what did you say?

What is the best thing that happened?

How will you make tomorrow awesome?

Doodle something fun:

Date:

Mood:

Song of the Day:

Name three things you're grateful for:

    1.

    2.

    3.

How was school today? And your extracurriculars?

Who did you compliment today? And what did you say?

What is the best thing that happened?

How will you make tomorrow awesome?

Doodle something fun:

Date:

Mood:

Song of the Day:

Name three things you're grateful for:

    1.

    2.

    3.

How was school today? And your extracurriculars?

Who did you compliment today? And what did you say?

What is the best thing that happened?

How will you make tomorrow awesome?

Doodle something fun:

Date:

Mood:

Song of the Day:

Name three things you're grateful for:

    1.

    2.

    3.

How was school today? And your extracurriculars?

Who did you compliment today? And what did you say?

What is the best thing that happened?

How will you make tomorrow awesome?

Doodle something fun:

Date:

Mood:

Song of the Day:

Name three things you're grateful for:

    1.

    2.

    3.

How was school today? And your extracurriculars?

Who did you compliment today? And what did you say?

What is the best thing that happened?

How will you make tomorrow awesome?

Doodle something fun:

Date:

Mood:

Song of the Day:

Name three things you're grateful for:

    1.

    2.

    3.

How was school today? And your extracurriculars?

Who did you compliment today? And what did you say?

What is the best thing that happened?

How will you make tomorrow awesome?

Doodle something fun:

Date:

Mood:

Song of the Day:

Name three things you're grateful for:

1.

2.

3.

How was school today? And your extracurriculars?

Who did you compliment today? And what did you say?

What is the best thing that happened?

How will you make tomorrow awesome?

Doodle something fun:

Date:

Mood:

Song of the Day:

Name three things you're grateful for:

    1.

    2.

    3.

How was school today? And your extracurriculars?

Who did you compliment today? And what did you say?

What is the best thing that happened?

How will you make tomorrow awesome?

Doodle something fun:

Date:

Mood:

Song of the Day:

Name three things you're grateful for:

    1.

    2.

    3.

How was school today? And your extracurriculars?

Who did you compliment today? And what did you say?

What is the best thing that happened?

How will you make tomorrow awesome?

Doodle something fun:

Date:

Mood:

Song of the Day:

Name three things you're grateful for:

    1.

    2.

    3.

How was school today? And your extracurriculars?

Who did you compliment today? And what did you say?

What is the best thing that happened?

How will you make tomorrow awesome?

Doodle something fun:

Date:

Mood:

Song of the Day:

Name three things you're grateful for:

   1.

   2.

   3.

How was school today? And your extracurriculars?

Who did you compliment today? And what did you say?

What is the best thing that happened?

How will you make tomorrow awesome?

Doodle something fun:

Date:

Mood:

Song of the Day:

Name three things you're grateful for:

    1.

    2.

    3.

How was school today? And your extracurriculars?

Who did you compliment today? And what did you say?

What is the best thing that happened?

How will you make tomorrow awesome?

Doodle something fun:

Date:

Mood:

Song of the Day:

Name three things you're grateful for:

    1.

    2.

    3.

How was school today? And your extracurriculars?

Who did you compliment today? And what did you say?

What is the best thing that happened?

How will you make tomorrow awesome?

Doodle something fun:

Date:

Mood:

Song of the Day:

Name three things you're grateful for:

    1.

    2.

    3.

How was school today? And your extracurriculars?

Who did you compliment today? And what did you say?

What is the best thing that happened?

How will you make tomorrow awesome?

Doodle something fun:

Date:

Mood:

Song of the Day:

Name three things you're grateful for:

    1.

    2.

    3.

How was school today? And your extracurriculars?

Who did you compliment today? And what did you say?

What is the best thing that happened?

How will you make tomorrow awesome?

Doodle something fun:

Date:

Mood:

Song of the Day:

Name three things you're grateful for:

    1.

    2.

    3.

How was school today? And your extracurriculars?

Who did you compliment today? And what did you say?

What is the best thing that happened?

How will you make tomorrow awesome?

Doodle something fun:

Date:

Mood:

Song of the Day:

Name three things you're grateful for:

    1.

    2.

    3.

How was school today? And your extracurriculars?

Who did you compliment today? And what did you say?

What is the best thing that happened?

How will you make tomorrow awesome?

Doodle something fun:

30-Day Check-In

Date:

Best thing that happened in the last 30 days:

Have you spent time working toward your goals?

How have your goals changed over the last 30 days?

Are you satisfied with the progress you've made?

How have you felt this month compared to last month?

What do you hope to accomplish in the next 30 days?

What can you do in the next 30 days to accomplish those things?

Date:

Mood:

Song of the Day:

Name three things you're grateful for:

    1.

    2.

    3.

How was school today? And your extracurriculars?

Who did you compliment today? And what did you say?

What is the best thing that happened?

How will you make tomorrow awesome?

Doodle something fun:

Date:

Mood:

Song of the Day:

Name three things you're grateful for:

    1.

    2.

    3.

How was school today? And your extracurriculars?

Who did you compliment today? And what did you say?

What is the best thing that happened?

How will you make tomorrow awesome?

Doodle something fun:

Date:

Mood:

Song of the Day:

Name three things you're grateful for:

    1.

    2.

    3.

How was school today? And your extracurriculars?

Who did you compliment today? And what did you say?

What is the best thing that happened?

How will you make tomorrow awesome?

Doodle something fun:

Date:

Mood:

Song of the Day:

Name three things you're grateful for:

    1.

    2.

    3.

How was school today? And your extracurriculars?

Who did you compliment today? And what did you say?

What is the best thing that happened?

How will you make tomorrow awesome?

Doodle something fun:

Date:

Mood:

Song of the Day:

Name three things you're grateful for:

1.

2.

3.

How was school today? And your extracurriculars?

Who did you compliment today? And what did you say?

What is the best thing that happened?

How will you make tomorrow awesome?

Doodle something fun:

Date:

Mood:

Song of the Day:

Name three things you're grateful for:

1.

2.

3.

How was school today? And your extracurriculars?

Who did you compliment today? And what did you say?

What is the best thing that happened?

How will you make tomorrow awesome?

Doodle something fun:

Date:

Mood:

Song of the Day:

Name three things you're grateful for:

    1.

    2.

    3.

How was school today? And your extracurriculars?

Who did you compliment today? And what did you say?

What is the best thing that happened?

How will you make tomorrow awesome?

Doodle something fun:

Date:

Mood:

Song of the Day:

Name three things you're grateful for:

1.

2.

3.

How was school today? And your extracurriculars?

Who did you compliment today? And what did you say?

What is the best thing that happened?

How will you make tomorrow awesome?

Doodle something fun:

Date:

Mood:

Song of the Day:

Name three things you're grateful for:

    1.

    2.

    3.

How was school today? And your extracurriculars?

Who did you compliment today? And what did you say?

What is the best thing that happened?

How will you make tomorrow awesome?

Doodle something fun:

Date:

Mood:

Song of the Day:

Name three things you're grateful for:

    1.

    2.

    3.

How was school today? And your extracurriculars?

Who did you compliment today? And what did you say?

What is the best thing that happened?

How will you make tomorrow awesome?

Doodle something fun:

Date:

Mood:

Song of the Day:

Name three things you're grateful for:

    1.

    2.

    3.

How was school today? And your extracurriculars?

Who did you compliment today? And what did you say?

What is the best thing that happened?

How will you make tomorrow awesome?

Doodle something fun:

Date:

Mood:

Song of the Day:

Name three things you're grateful for:

    1.

    2.

    3.

How was school today? And your extracurriculars?

Who did you compliment today? And what did you say?

What is the best thing that happened?

How will you make tomorrow awesome?

Doodle something fun:

Date:

Mood:

Song of the Day:

Name three things you're grateful for:

1.

2.

3.

How was school today? And your extracurriculars?

Who did you compliment today? And what did you say?

What is the best thing that happened?

How will you make tomorrow awesome?

Doodle something fun:

Date:

Mood:

Song of the Day:

Name three things you're grateful for:

    1.

    2.

    3.

How was school today? And your extracurriculars?

Who did you compliment today? And what did you say?

What is the best thing that happened?

How will you make tomorrow awesome?

Doodle something fun:

Date:

Mood:

Song of the Day:

Name three things you're grateful for:

    1.

    2.

    3.

How was school today? And your extracurriculars?

Who did you compliment today? And what did you say?

What is the best thing that happened?

How will you make tomorrow awesome?

Doodle something fun:

Date:

Mood:

Song of the Day:

Name three things you're grateful for:

1.

2.

3.

How was school today? And your extracurriculars?

Who did you compliment today? And what did you say?

What is the best thing that happened?

How will you make tomorrow awesome?

Doodle something fun:

Date:

Mood:

Song of the Day:

Name three things you're grateful for:

    1.

    2.

    3.

How was school today? And your extracurriculars?

Who did you compliment today? And what did you say?

What is the best thing that happened?

How will you make tomorrow awesome?

Doodle something fun:

Date:

Mood:

Song of the Day:

Name three things you're grateful for:

1.

2.

3.

How was school today? And your extracurriculars?

Who did you compliment today? And what did you say?

What is the best thing that happened?

How will you make tomorrow awesome?

Doodle something fun:

Date:

Mood:

Song of the Day:

Name three things you're grateful for:

    1.

    2.

    3.

How was school today? And your extracurriculars?

Who did you compliment today? And what did you say?

What is the best thing that happened?

How will you make tomorrow awesome?

Doodle something fun:

Date:

Mood:

Song of the Day:

Name three things you're grateful for:

    1.

    2.

    3.

How was school today? And your extracurriculars?

Who did you compliment today? And what did you say?

What is the best thing that happened?

How will you make tomorrow awesome?

Doodle something fun:

Date:

Mood:

Song of the Day:

Name three things you're grateful for:

    1.

    2.

    3.

How was school today? And your extracurriculars?

Who did you compliment today? And what did you say?

What is the best thing that happened?

How will you make tomorrow awesome?

Doodle something fun:

Date:

Mood:

Song of the Day:

Name three things you're grateful for:

    1.

    2.

    3.

How was school today? And your extracurriculars?

Who did you compliment today? And what did you say?

What is the best thing that happened?

How will you make tomorrow awesome?

Doodle something fun:

Date:

Mood:

Song of the Day:

Name three things you're grateful for:

    1.

    2.

    3.

How was school today? And your extracurriculars?

Who did you compliment today? And what did you say?

What is the best thing that happened?

How will you make tomorrow awesome?

Doodle something fun:

Date:

Mood:

Song of the Day:

Name three things you're grateful for:

    1.

    2.

    3.

How was school today? And your extracurriculars?

Who did you compliment today? And what did you say?

What is the best thing that happened?

How will you make tomorrow awesome?

Doodle something fun:

Date:

Mood:

Song of the Day:

Name three things you're grateful for:

    1.

    2.

    3.

How was school today? And your extracurriculars?

Who did you compliment today? And what did you say?

What is the best thing that happened?

How will you make tomorrow awesome?

Doodle something fun:

Date:

Mood:

Song of the Day:

Name three things you're grateful for:

    1.

    2.

    3.

How was school today? And your extracurriculars?

Who did you compliment today? And what did you say?

What is the best thing that happened?

How will you make tomorrow awesome?

Doodle something fun:

Date:

Mood:

Song of the Day:

Name three things you're grateful for:

    1.

    2.

    3.

How was school today? And your extracurriculars?

Who did you compliment today? And what did you say?

What is the best thing that happened?

How will you make tomorrow awesome?

Doodle something fun:

Date:

Mood:

Song of the Day:

Name three things you're grateful for:

    1.

    2.

    3.

How was school today? And your extracurriculars?

Who did you compliment today? And what did you say?

What is the best thing that happened?

How will you make tomorrow awesome?

Doodle something fun:

Date:

Mood:

Song of the Day:

Name three things you're grateful for:

    1.

    2.

    3.

How was school today? And your extracurriculars?

Who did you compliment today? And what did you say?

What is the best thing that happened?

How will you make tomorrow awesome?

Doodle something fun:

Date:

Mood:

Song of the Day:

Name three things you're grateful for:

    1.

    2.

    3.

How was school today? And your extracurriculars?

Who did you compliment today? And what did you say?

What is the best thing that happened?

How will you make tomorrow awesome?

Doodle something fun:

30-Day Check-In

Date:

Best thing that happened in the last 30 days:

Have you spent time working toward your goals?

How have your goals changed over the last 30 days?

Are you satisfied with the progress you've made?

How have you felt this month compared to last month?

What do you hope to accomplish in the next 30 days?

What can you do in the next 30 days to accomplish those things?

Date:

Mood:

Song of the Day:

Name three things you're grateful for:

1.

2.

3.

How was school today? And your extracurriculars?

Who did you compliment today? And what did you say?

What is the best thing that happened?

How will you make tomorrow awesome?

Doodle something fun:

Date:

Mood:

Song of the Day:

Name three things you're grateful for:

　　1.

　　2.

　　3.

How was school today? And your extracurriculars?

Who did you compliment today? And what did you say?

What is the best thing that happened?

How will you make tomorrow awesome?

Doodle something fun:

Date:

Mood:

Song of the Day:

Name three things you're grateful for:

    1.

    2.

    3.

How was school today? And your extracurriculars?

Who did you compliment today? And what did you say?

What is the best thing that happened?

How will you make tomorrow awesome?

Doodle something fun:

Date:

Mood:

Song of the Day:

Name three things you're grateful for:

    1.

    2.

    3.

How was school today? And your extracurriculars?

Who did you compliment today? And what did you say?

What is the best thing that happened?

How will you make tomorrow awesome?

Doodle something fun:

Date:

Mood:

Song of the Day:

Name three things you're grateful for:

    1.

    2.

    3.

How was school today? And your extracurriculars?

Who did you compliment today? And what did you say?

What is the best thing that happened?

How will you make tomorrow awesome?

Doodle something fun:

Date:

Mood:

Song of the Day:

Name three things you're grateful for:

    1.

    2.

    3.

How was school today? And your extracurriculars?

Who did you compliment today? And what did you say?

What is the best thing that happened?

How will you make tomorrow awesome?

Doodle something fun:

Date:

Mood:

Song of the Day:

Name three things you're grateful for:

    1.

    2.

    3.

How was school today? And your extracurriculars?

Who did you compliment today? And what did you say?

What is the best thing that happened?

How will you make tomorrow awesome?

Doodle something fun:

Date:

Mood:

Song of the Day:

Name three things you're grateful for:

    1.

    2.

    3.

How was school today? And your extracurriculars?

Who did you compliment today? And what did you say?

What is the best thing that happened?

How will you make tomorrow awesome?

Doodle something fun:

Date:

Mood:

Song of the Day:

Name three things you're grateful for:

1.

2.

3.

How was school today? And your extracurriculars?

Who did you compliment today? And what did you say?

What is the best thing that happened?

How will you make tomorrow awesome?

Doodle something fun:

Date:

Mood:

Song of the Day:

Name three things you're grateful for:

    1.

    2.

    3.

How was school today? And your extracurriculars?

Who did you compliment today? And what did you say?

What is the best thing that happened?

How will you make tomorrow awesome?

Doodle something fun:

Date:

Mood:

Song of the Day:

Name three things you're grateful for:

    1.

    2.

    3.

How was school today? And your extracurriculars?

Who did you compliment today? And what did you say?

What is the best thing that happened?

How will you make tomorrow awesome?

Doodle something fun:

Date:

Mood:

Song of the Day:

Name three things you're grateful for:

    1.

    2.

    3.

How was school today? And your extracurriculars?

Who did you compliment today? And what did you say?

What is the best thing that happened?

How will you make tomorrow awesome?

Doodle something fun:

Date:

Mood:

Song of the Day:

Name three things you're grateful for:

    1.

    2.

    3.

How was school today? And your extracurriculars?

Who did you compliment today? And what did you say?

What is the best thing that happened?

How will you make tomorrow awesome?

Doodle something fun:

Date:

Mood:

Song of the Day:

Name three things you're grateful for:

    1.

    2.

    3.

How was school today? And your extracurriculars?

Who did you compliment today? And what did you say?

What is the best thing that happened?

How will you make tomorrow awesome?

Doodle something fun:

Date:

Mood:

Song of the Day:

Name three things you're grateful for:

    1.

    2.

    3.

How was school today? And your extracurriculars?

Who did you compliment today? And what did you say?

What is the best thing that happened?

How will you make tomorrow awesome?

Doodle something fun:

Date:

Mood:

Song of the Day:

Name three things you're grateful for:

    1.

    2.

    3.

How was school today? And your extracurriculars?

Who did you compliment today? And what did you say?

What is the best thing that happened?

How will you make tomorrow awesome?

Doodle something fun:

Date:

Mood:

Song of the Day:

Name three things you're grateful for:

    1.

    2.

    3.

How was school today? And your extracurriculars?

Who did you compliment today? And what did you say?

What is the best thing that happened?

How will you make tomorrow awesome?

Doodle something fun:

Date:

Mood:

Song of the Day:

Name three things you're grateful for:

1.

2.

3.

How was school today? And your extracurriculars?

Who did you compliment today? And what did you say?

What is the best thing that happened?

How will you make tomorrow awesome?

Doodle something fun:

Date:

Mood:

Song of the Day:

Name three things you're grateful for:

    1.

    2.

    3.

How was school today? And your extracurriculars?

Who did you compliment today? And what did you say?

What is the best thing that happened?

How will you make tomorrow awesome?

Doodle something fun:

Date:

Mood:

Song of the Day:

Name three things you're grateful for:

    1.

    2.

    3.

How was school today? And your extracurriculars?

Who did you compliment today? And what did you say?

What is the best thing that happened?

How will you make tomorrow awesome?

Doodle something fun:

Date:

Mood:

Song of the Day:

Name three things you're grateful for:

    1.

    2.

    3.

How was school today? And your extracurriculars?

Who did you compliment today? And what did you say?

What is the best thing that happened?

How will you make tomorrow awesome?

Doodle something fun:

Date:

Mood:

Song of the Day:

Name three things you're grateful for:

    1.

    2.

    3.

How was school today? And your extracurriculars?

Who did you compliment today? And what did you say?

What is the best thing that happened?

How will you make tomorrow awesome?

Doodle something fun:

Date:

Mood:

Song of the Day:

Name three things you're grateful for:

1.

2.

3.

How was school today? And your extracurriculars?

Who did you compliment today? And what did you say?

What is the best thing that happened?

How will you make tomorrow awesome?

Doodle something fun:

Date:

Mood:

Song of the Day:

Name three things you're grateful for:

    1.

    2.

    3.

How was school today? And your extracurriculars?

Who did you compliment today? And what did you say?

What is the best thing that happened?

How will you make tomorrow awesome?

Doodle something fun:

Date:

Mood:

Song of the Day:

Name three things you're grateful for:

    1.

    2.

    3.

How was school today? And your extracurriculars?

Who did you compliment today? And what did you say?

What is the best thing that happened?

How will you make tomorrow awesome?

Doodle something fun:

Date:

Mood:

Song of the Day:

Name three things you're grateful for:

    1.

    2.

    3.

How was school today? And your extracurriculars?

Who did you compliment today? And what did you say?

What is the best thing that happened?

How will you make tomorrow awesome?

Doodle something fun:

Date:

Mood:

Song of the Day:

Name three things you're grateful for:

1.

2.

3.

How was school today? And your extracurriculars?

Who did you compliment today? And what did you say?

What is the best thing that happened?

How will you make tomorrow awesome?

Doodle something fun:

Date:

Mood:

Song of the Day:

Name three things you're grateful for:

    1.

    2.

    3.

How was school today? And your extracurriculars?

Who did you compliment today? And what did you say?

What is the best thing that happened?

How will you make tomorrow awesome?

Doodle something fun:

Date:

Mood:

Song of the Day:

Name three things you're grateful for:

    1.

    2.

    3.

How was school today? And your extracurriculars?

Who did you compliment today? And what did you say?

What is the best thing that happened?

How will you make tomorrow awesome?

Doodle something fun:

Date:

Mood:

Song of the Day:

Name three things you're grateful for:

    1.

    2.

    3.

How was school today? And your extracurriculars?

Who did you compliment today? And what did you say?

What is the best thing that happened?

How will you make tomorrow awesome?

Doodle something fun:

30-Day Check-In

Date:

Best thing that happened in the last 30 days:

Have you spent time working toward your goals?

How have your goals changed over the last 30 days?

Are you satisfied with the progress you've made?

How have you felt this month compared to last month?

What do you hope to accomplish in the next 30 days?

What can you do in the next 30 days to accomplish those things?

Date:

Mood:

Song of the Day:

Name three things you're grateful for:

    1.

    2.

    3.

How was school today? And your extracurriculars?

Who did you compliment today? And what did you say?

What is the best thing that happened?

How will you make tomorrow awesome?

Doodle something fun:

Date:

Mood:

Song of the Day:

Name three things you're grateful for:

1.

2.

3.

How was school today? And your extracurriculars?

Who did you compliment today? And what did you say?

What is the best thing that happened?

How will you make tomorrow awesome?

Doodle something fun:

Date:

Mood:

Song of the Day:

Name three things you're grateful for:

    1.

    2.

    3.

How was school today? And your extracurriculars?

Who did you compliment today? And what did you say?

What is the best thing that happened?

How will you make tomorrow awesome?

Doodle something fun:

Date:

Mood:

Song of the Day:

Name three things you're grateful for:

1.

2.

3.

How was school today? And your extracurriculars?

Who did you compliment today? And what did you say?

What is the best thing that happened?

How will you make tomorrow awesome?

Doodle something fun:

Date:

Mood:

Song of the Day:

Name three things you're grateful for:

   1.

   2.

   3.

How was school today? And your extracurriculars?

Who did you compliment today? And what did you say?

What is the best thing that happened?

How will you make tomorrow awesome?

Doodle something fun:

Date:

Mood:

Song of the Day:

Name three things you're grateful for:

    1.

    2.

    3.

How was school today? And your extracurriculars?

Who did you compliment today? And what did you say?

What is the best thing that happened?

How will you make tomorrow awesome?

Doodle something fun:

Date:

Mood:

Song of the Day:

Name three things you're grateful for:

    1.

    2.

    3.

How was school today? And your extracurriculars?

Who did you compliment today? And what did you say?

What is the best thing that happened?

How will you make tomorrow awesome?

Doodle something fun:

Date:

Mood:

Song of the Day:

Name three things you're grateful for:

    1.

    2.

    3.

How was school today? And your extracurriculars?

Who did you compliment today? And what did you say?

What is the best thing that happened?

How will you make tomorrow awesome?

Doodle something fun:

Date:

Mood:

Song of the Day:

Name three things you're grateful for:

    1.

    2.

    3.

How was school today? And your extracurriculars?

Who did you compliment today? And what did you say?

What is the best thing that happened?

How will you make tomorrow awesome?

Doodle something fun:

Date:

Mood:

Song of the Day:

Name three things you're grateful for:

    1.

    2.

    3.

How was school today? And your extracurriculars?

Who did you compliment today? And what did you say?

What is the best thing that happened?

How will you make tomorrow awesome?

Doodle something fun:

Date:

Mood:

Song of the Day:

Name three things you're grateful for:

    1.

    2.

    3.

How was school today? And your extracurriculars?

Who did you compliment today? And what did you say?

What is the best thing that happened?

How will you make tomorrow awesome?

Doodle something fun:

Date:

Mood:

Song of the Day:

Name three things you're grateful for:

1.

2.

3.

How was school today? And your extracurriculars?

Who did you compliment today? And what did you say?

What is the best thing that happened?

How will you make tomorrow awesome?

Doodle something fun:

Date:

Mood:

Song of the Day:

Name three things you're grateful for:

    1.

    2.

    3.

How was school today? And your extracurriculars?

Who did you compliment today? And what did you say?

What is the best thing that happened?

How will you make tomorrow awesome?

Doodle something fun:

Date:

Mood:

Song of the Day:

Name three things you're grateful for:

1.

2.

3.

How was school today? And your extracurriculars?

Who did you compliment today? And what did you say?

What is the best thing that happened?

How will you make tomorrow awesome?

Doodle something fun:

Date:

Mood:

Song of the Day:

Name three things you're grateful for:

    1.

    2.

    3.

How was school today? And your extracurriculars?

Who did you compliment today? And what did you say?

What is the best thing that happened?

How will you make tomorrow awesome?

Doodle something fun:

Date:

Mood:

Song of the Day:

Name three things you're grateful for:

1.

2.

3.

How was school today? And your extracurriculars?

Who did you compliment today? And what did you say?

What is the best thing that happened?

How will you make tomorrow awesome?

Doodle something fun:

Date:

Mood:

Song of the Day:

Name three things you're grateful for:

    1.

    2.

    3.

How was school today? And your extracurriculars?

Who did you compliment today? And what did you say?

What is the best thing that happened?

How will you make tomorrow awesome?

Doodle something fun:

Date:

Mood:

Song of the Day:

Name three things you're grateful for:

    1.

    2.

    3.

How was school today? And your extracurriculars?

Who did you compliment today? And what did you say?

What is the best thing that happened?

How will you make tomorrow awesome?

Doodle something fun:

Date:

Mood:

Song of the Day:

Name three things you're grateful for:

    1.

    2.

    3.

How was school today? And your extracurriculars?

Who did you compliment today? And what did you say?

What is the best thing that happened?

How will you make tomorrow awesome?

Doodle something fun:

Date:

Mood:

Song of the Day:

Name three things you're grateful for:

    1.

    2.

    3.

How was school today? And your extracurriculars?

Who did you compliment today? And what did you say?

What is the best thing that happened?

How will you make tomorrow awesome?

Doodle something fun:

Date:

Mood:

Song of the Day:

Name three things you're grateful for:

    1.

    2.

    3.

How was school today? And your extracurriculars?

Who did you compliment today? And what did you say?

What is the best thing that happened?

How will you make tomorrow awesome?

Doodle something fun:

Date:

Mood:

Song of the Day:

Name three things you're grateful for:

    1.

    2.

    3.

How was school today? And your extracurriculars?

Who did you compliment today? And what did you say?

What is the best thing that happened?

How will you make tomorrow awesome?

Doodle something fun:

Date:

Mood:

Song of the Day:

Name three things you're grateful for:

    1.

    2.

    3.

How was school today? And your extracurriculars?

Who did you compliment today? And what did you say?

What is the best thing that happened?

How will you make tomorrow awesome?

Doodle something fun:

Date:

Mood:

Song of the Day:

Name three things you're grateful for:

    1.

    2.

    3.

How was school today? And your extracurriculars?

Who did you compliment today? And what did you say?

What is the best thing that happened?

How will you make tomorrow awesome?

Doodle something fun:

Date:

Mood:

Song of the Day:

Name three things you're grateful for:

    1.

    2.

    3.

How was school today? And your extracurriculars?

Who did you compliment today? And what did you say?

What is the best thing that happened?

How will you make tomorrow awesome?

Doodle something fun:

Date:

Mood:

Song of the Day:

Name three things you're grateful for:

    1.

    2.

    3.

How was school today? And your extracurriculars?

Who did you compliment today? And what did you say?

What is the best thing that happened?

How will you make tomorrow awesome?

Doodle something fun:

Date:

Mood:

Song of the Day:

Name three things you're grateful for:

    1.

    2.

    3.

How was school today? And your extracurriculars?

Who did you compliment today? And what did you say?

What is the best thing that happened?

How will you make tomorrow awesome?

Doodle something fun:

Date:

Mood:

Song of the Day:

Name three things you're grateful for:

1.

2.

3.

How was school today? And your extracurriculars?

Who did you compliment today? And what did you say?

What is the best thing that happened?

How will you make tomorrow awesome?

Doodle something fun:

Date:

Mood:

Song of the Day:

Name three things you're grateful for:

    1.

    2.

    3.

How was school today? And your extracurriculars?

Who did you compliment today? And what did you say?

What is the best thing that happened?

How will you make tomorrow awesome?

Doodle something fun:

Date:

Mood:

Song of the Day:

Name three things you're grateful for:

    1.

    2.

    3.

How was school today? And your extracurriculars?

Who did you compliment today? And what did you say?

What is the best thing that happened?

How will you make tomorrow awesome?

Doodle something fun:

30-Day Check-In

Date:

Best thing that happened in the last 30 days:

Have you spent time working toward your goals?

How have your goals changed over the last 30 days?

Are you satisfied with the progress you've made?

How have you felt this month compared to last month?

What do you hope to accomplish in the next 30 days?

What can you do in the next 30 days to accomplish those things?

Notes or Doodles

Notes or Doodles

Notes or Doodles

Notes or Doodles

Notes or Doodles

Notes or Doodles

ABOUT THE AUTHOR

Mickey Reed is the author of positivity, kindness, and productivity journals and workbooks. She's also a fiction writer (Eliza Boyd), avid reader, editor, wife, pet mom, stepmom, blogger (Fruit So Hard), vegan, positivity warrior, and addict of dessert. When she's not reading, writing, or spreading a positive message, she's likely doing yoga, snuggling her dogs, posting photos on Instagram, or binge-watching something with Husband.

Have thoughts, questions, suggestions, or comments about the journal? Mickey would love to hear from you! Feel free to find her on any of her social media sites.

Website: www.mickeyreedjournals.com

Facebook: www.facebook.com/mickeyreedjournals

Twitter: www.twitter.com/mreedjournals

Instagram: www.instagram.com/mickeyreedjournals

Pinterest: www.pinterest.com/mickeyreedjournals

Newsletter: http://bit.ly/2FKjE0N

Find other editions of this journal: www.amazon.com/author/mickeyreed

And join other journal users in the official Facebook group: www.facebook.com/groups/mickeyreedjournals/

Made in the USA
Columbia, SC
12 June 2019